PARENTING *for Beginners*

PARENTING 101

PARENTING

for Beginners

CLIVE WHICHELOW

ILLUSTRATIONS BY IAN BAKER

summersdale

PARENTING FOR BEGINNERS

Summersdale Publishers Ltd
46 West Street
Chichester
West Sussex
PO19 1RP
UK

www.summersdale.com

Printed and bound in China

ISBN: 978-1-84953-836-7

Substantial discounts on bulk quantities of Summersdale books are available to corporations, professional associations and other organisations. For details contact Nicky Douglas by telephone: +44 (0) 1243 756902, fax: +44 (0) 1243 786300 or email: nicky@summersdale.com.

INTRODUCTION

Well, how hard can it be really? Parenting has been going on since Adam and Eve. OK, so they were making it up as they went along when they became parents, but this parenting lark isn't exactly new. You'd think we'd have got it right by now, wouldn't you?

But every time people are about to become parents for the first time they get a bit anxious and start asking the important questions: how long before I can I start drinking wine again? Should the father be there at the birth – especially if he can barely remember being there at the conception? Why do nappies cost so much?

Yes, from the moment a woman announces she is pregnant – and the moment the man picks himself up off the floor again – the questions start and they don't really stop until the kids are grown up. Actually, they continue even then: when are they going to give us our first grandchild? Why are they still borrowing money off us? And will they *ever* move out of our house?

But perhaps we should mainly concern ourselves with parenting from the time they are born until the time they are teenagers – from the cradle to the rave, you might say.

One word of comfort: all new parents are beginners – join the club!

THINGS YOU'LL SUDDENLY REALISE DURING PREGNANCY

You have had absolutely no training for the most important job of your life

A woman has to be at least eight months gone before anyone offers up their bus seat

This baby is going to cost you a small fortune

You can't delay the birth
till you're better prepared

ADVICE FOR DADS-TO-BE ATTENDING THE BIRTH

Don't give your partner any advice – she knows darn well you've never had to do it

After several hours, the constant brow-mopping can get a bit irritating

Try to forget about what you're missing on TV

Your partner wants support and encouragement, not regular bursts of applause

THINGS YOU'LL FIND OUT SOON AFTER THE BIRTH

Everyone will want to see the new baby
– it will take you half an hour to walk
from one end of your road to the other

The baby won't necessarily share your
view that 3 a.m. is a time when all
normal people should be fast asleep

Two hours' uninterrupted sleep will
seem like a gift from Heaven

You can't just spontaneously pop down the pub for a quick one any more

BABY NAMES YOU MIGHT WANT TO RECONSIDER

Messi

★

Juan Direction

★

Chewbacca

★

Baby Gaga

WAYS TO SAVE
A FORTUNE

The baby won't care if you buy
a designer buggy or not, so get a
normal one – they go just as fast

Babies have this habit of growing,
so expensive baby clothes might
only be worn about three times
(like some of mum's outfits!)

You could buy washable nappies
– OK, maybe disposables are
a worthwhile expense!

Does your little one really
need baby yoga/pilates/
taekwondo lessons?

UPSIDES AND DOWNSIDES OF PARENTING

UPSIDES	DOWNSIDES
You get to reread all your favourite children's books	After the 200th time even your favourite story starts to wear a bit thin
You can have a sneaky go on the swings in the playground	Your body isn't quite up to sudden movements any more
You can watch them grow and develop	Before long they're bigger than you and answering back
You'll make lots of new friends through them	You also have to put up with pushy parents, playground politics and endless involvement in school fundraising

WAYS YOU PROBABLY SHOULDN'T TRY TO SAVE MONEY

Using disposable nappies more than once

Strapping the baby on the roof rack
instead of buying a car seat

Making their birthday parties 'bring
your own jelly and ice cream'

Using a supermarket trolley
instead of a baby buggy

UPSIDES AND DOWNSIDES OF NANNIES

UPSIDES	DOWNSIDES
They give you a bit of free time	The kids might struggle to remember who exactly you are
They have time for lots of fun activities	The kids wonder why the hell you can't make upside-down cakes, perform puppet theatre or teach juggling
They're usually younger than you and have lots of energy	They make you feel like a knackered old crone
They become like part of the family	They then get headhunted by some couple at school that you can't stand

WAYS IN WHICH CHILD SAFETY MEASURES COULD BACKFIRE

You too might find it impossible to open the cupboard under the sink where the bleach is stored

In a sleepy daze you might forget that there's a gate at the top of the stairs and arrive at the breakfast table far sooner than anticipated

You might be tempted to put so many precious and valuable items out of harm's way your house will look as bare as a padded cell

FOOD YOUR NEWBORN BABY MIGHT NOT BE QUITE READY FOR YET

Big Macs

Quinoa

Lobster thermidor

Battered Mars bars

KIDS' TOYS AND WHERE THEY CAN LEAD

Toy money – your child becoming a
rogue trader on the stock exchange

Train set – your child becoming
a militant trade-union leader

Wendy house – your child becoming
a dodgy property developer

Rocking horse – a small
fortune in real riding lessons
by the time they're ten

HOW KIDS MAY CHALLENGE THOSE OLD WIVES' TALES

'If carrots help you see in the dark, why don't rabbits come out at night?'

'If eating greens makes you big and strong, why don't gerbils look like Superman?'

'If you'll "stay like that" when crossing your eyes, why aren't most adults cross-eyed?'

SIGNS THAT YOU MAY HAVE TO RETHINK THIS PARENTING LARK

You're trying to decide where exactly baby should have his or her first tattoo

You're hunting for a baby smartphone

You've fitted your baby alarm with a snooze button

You can't decide whether the baby should be named after all the members of Mum's favourite football team or Dad's

SONGS FOR NEW PARENTS

'Baby Love'

'Crying'

'All Night Long'

'A Change Is Gonna Come'

THINGS TO REMEMBER WHEN THE GOING GETS TOUGH

At some point they will sleep right
through the night – and so will you!

They won't always be sick over your
shoulder – they like to vary it a bit

You are doing a fantastic job –
especially considering you've had
absolutely no training at all

One day they will thank you
for all this – well, they probably
won't but it's a nice thought!

THE DIFFERENCES BETWEEN BRINGING UP BABIES AND BRINGING UP TEENAGERS

BABIES	TEENAGERS
Babies get stroppy and you don't know why	Teenagers get stroppy and they don't know why
Babies keep you up half the night with you wondering if they'll ever get to sleep	Teenagers keep you up half the night with you wondering if they'll ever come home
Babies communicate in non-verbal language and gesticulations	So do some teenagers – no difference there then!
Babies can exist on an entirely liquid diet	So can teenagers – with perhaps the occasional bit of junk food thrown in

THINGS NOT TO DO FOR A KIDS' BIRTHDAY PARTY

Hire a professional entertainer
– all the other parents will hate
you for 'upping the ante'

Let the other parents stay for 'a glass' of
wine – you don't want to have to deal
with adults being sick as well as children

Make loads of healthy food – it will
remain untouched as they ravenously
devour every last crisp, biscuit and sweet

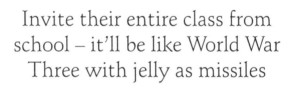

Invite their entire class from
school – it'll be like World War
Three with jelly as missiles

THINGS YOU SHOULD CONSIDER FOR A KIDS' BIRTHDAY PARTY

Have a definite end time – or the other parents will see you as a free babysitting service

Confine them to one room – it's embarrassing to be still finding odd children dotted round the house three days later

Warn the neighbours, who will otherwise assume you are being burgled by a gang of banshees

THINGS YOU'LL HAVE TO REMEMBER HOW TO DO AGAIN

Make a cat's cradle

Make a kazoo noise with a blade
of grass between your hands

Make a daisy chain

Play 'This Little Piggy'

HOW TO SPOT AN OVERPROTECTIVE PARENT

They have a 'Baby on Board'
sticker on the pram

The baby wears water wings in the bath

The legs have been sawn off the high chair

The baby has a mini Zimmer frame
while it's learning to walk

YOU'RE A PUSHY PARENT IF...

You put your child's name down for
Eton before they were conceived

You insist on having the other kids
drug-tested on school sports day

You have a spreadsheet showing if all their
party invitations have been reciprocated

You insist that their home tutors
have honours degrees

HOW A PARENT'S ROLE CHANGES

TODDLERS	TEENAGERS
You're someone who knows everything	You're now someone who knows nothing
You're someone who's big and strong	You someone who seems to be getting smaller by the day
You're someone to have fun with	You're someone who stops them from having fun
You're a shoulder to cry on	You're still a shoulder to cry on – some things never change!

THINGS YOU CAN LEARN FROM YOUR OWN PARENTS

Parents are a constant source
of embarrassment however
young/cool they are (or think they are)

Parents do not understand
the modern world

You can safely ignore any advice
parents give you – until it turns
out to have been right all along

However old you are, the
Bank of Mum and Dad is
still open for business

LAST-DITCH LULLABIES YOU MIGHT WANT TO TRY

'Shaddap You Face'

* * *

'Give Peace a Chance'

* * *

'Silence Is Golden'

* * *

'Stop Your Sobbing'

SKILLS YOU MUST NOW MASTER

Being able to maintain a fixed smile
while your two-year-old jumps onto
your stomach from the arm of the sofa

Laughing heartily at a 'joke' told
to you by your four-year-old that
makes no sense whatsoever

Finding reserves of patience in situations
that would have a saint tearing his hair out

Being able to fold and stow a buggy in three seconds flat

A DAD'S GUIDE TO DAUGHTERS

They want to be just like Mummy
– until they're teenagers, then
that's the last thing they want

They learn to twist men round
their little fingers from an early
age – starting with Dad!

They regard boys as nasty, smelly, revolting
creatures until they discover boy bands

A MUM'S GUIDE
TO SONS

They want to be just like Daddy – until
they take an interest in fashion and
realise that dad leaves a lot to be desired

Boys do love getting dirty – they
are basically the main reason that
washing machines were invented

They regard girls as soppy, silly,
wimpish little creatures – until
they discover that teenage girls are
an entirely different species

THINGS YOU'LL LAUGH ABOUT LATER (HONEST!)

Trying to rock the baby to sleep at 4 a.m.

Finding half-sucked rusks in your
work suit pockets (at work)

Trying to feed a baby that stubbornly
refuses to open its mouth

Noticing in the washroom mirror at work
that you have porridge in your hair

CHANGES IN YOUR ROUTINE WHEN YOU HAVE A BABY

You won't need that alarm clock any more!

You will probably each have to
eat your dinner in shifts

You will look forward to rare nights
out together as a weight-watcher looks
forward to an illicit bar of chocolate

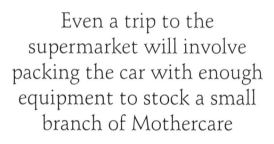

Even a trip to the supermarket will involve packing the car with enough equipment to stock a small branch of Mothercare

THINGS YOU NEVER THOUGHT YOU'D HAVE TO DO

Wipe someone else's bottom

Pay someone so you can go out for a meal

Actually get into a conversation
about breast versus bottle

Start writing to Father Christmas again

HOW TO SPOT ANOTHER NEW PARENT

They are still wearing the same clothes they had on three days ago

Their clothes are covered in baby food and various other unidentifiable stains

Despite everything they still have a big, soppy grin on their faces

They wander around
in a sleep-deprived daze
that makes a zombie look
bright-eyed and bushy-tailed

THINGS TO LOOK FORWARD TO

The day someone asks your advice
on parenting – yes, before long you
will be considered an expert!

The first time baby sleeps right
through the night – and it'll be
your first time for a while too!

You can become a big kid again yourself –
building sandcastles, watching cartoons,
scoffing sweets… What's not to like?

One day, far in the future, your
children might be looking after you!

SNAPPY ANSWERS
TO KIDS' QUESTIONS

Why is the sky blue?
It's feeling a bit fed up

Where do babies come from?
Never mind where they come
from; where do they go?

What is infinity?
It's the time it takes someone to
answer the phone at the doctors

SIGNS YOU MAY BE
SPOILING THEM

The party bags you give out resemble
goody bags at Oscars night

They had riding lessons
before they could walk

Their godparents are members
of the royal family

Their toy cars have personalised
number plates

FRIENDSHIPS YOU SHOULD ENCOURAGE

That child in their class whose parents have a villa in Barbados

The child in their class who actually likes spinach and broccoli

The child that just happens to be related to the head teacher

The child whose parents
have a swimming pool
in their back garden

OTHER THINGS PTA MIGHT STAND FOR

People To Avoid

Planning Takes Ages

Please Take Advantage!

Persuaded To Assist

CHILDREN YOU MAY NOT WANT YOUR OWN TO MIX WITH

The one whose parents are tax inspectors

The ones who give such expensive
birthday presents to your kids you
end up spending a fortune on theirs

The one who thinks 'parental advisory'
on an album means his parents
have advised him to listen to it

The one who seems to
think head lice are pets

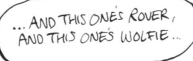

WHAT YOUR KIDS WILL WANT AND WHAT THEY MAYBE SHOULD HAVE

WILL WANT	SHOULD HAVE
Lashings of sweets	Rations of sweets
Clothes with designer labels	Clothes with sewn-in name labels
Regular trips to Disneyland	Regular trips to Poundland
Meals without greens	Meals without moaning

SIGNS YOUR CHILD MIGHT BE A GENIUS

They prefer chess to draughts – or perhaps it's because chess has a 'horsey'

They seem fascinated by *University Challenge* – though it could be they just wonder how one team sits on top of the other one without falling off

They want to stay up for *Question Time* – or maybe it's just because it's on really late

In the newsagents they go straight for the *Financial Times* – or maybe it's just because they like pink

UPDATED GAMES FOR THE MODERN CHILD

Visually-impaired Person's Buff

Cops and People Driven to
Anti-social Behaviour

I Spy With My Little Drone

A PARENTS' GUIDE TO HOMEWORK

Only help your kids if you're prepared to get an embarrassingly low mark

Whichever way you did maths in your day, it is now hopelessly out of date

'The dog ate my homework' excuse has now been superseded by 'My laptop crashed'

There are two types of child in secondary school: those who are given homework – and fibbers

THE PROS AND CONS OF PRIVATE SCHOOLING

PROS	CONS
They will mix with a higher class of children	They will get so posh they will disown you
They will have smaller class sizes	You will have a smaller bank balance
They will get a first-class education	You will have no hope of being able to help them with their homework
They will have the opportunity to go on fantastic school trips	You will have to work all the hours under the sun to pay for them

CHILDREN'S CLAIMS YOU MIGHT WANT TO DISTRUST

'The fairies gave my friend
£20 for her tooth'

'Fresh fruit has been banned
from our school lunchboxes'

'All my friends have got the latest iPhone'

'For my homework I have
to research video games'

SIGNS YOU MAY HAVE TO IMPROVE YOUR PARENTING SKILLS

Your kids have got Childline on speed dial

For their birthday they request suitcases and one-way airline tickets

Not only do they not believe in Father Christmas, they've never heard of him

You find they've locked the front door when you roll home from the pub

SCHOOL TRIPS – WHAT YOU NEED TO KNOW

However much food you put in their packed lunch, it will all be scoffed in the first 10 minutes on the coach

If they take a camera, don't expect any fascinating shots of where they've actually been, but a montage of pictures of their mates gurning at the camera

If you say 'yes' to all the school trips they're offered, you'll need a medium-sized lottery win to fund it all

Whereas your school trips
used to involve going to the
Tower of London or the local
museum, theirs might involve
the Taj Mahal or the pyramids

THINGS TO REMEMBER WHEN GETTING KIDS TO HELP OUT ROUND THE HOUSE

They know that the more crockery they break when washing up will mean the less to wash up next time

Tidying their bedroom should not mean simply rearranging all the contents into different positions around the room

If they help with dinner, be sure to have a fire extinguisher ready at hand

SLEEPOVERS – WHAT YOU SHOULD KNOW

Sleepovers don't actually
involve much sleep

Beware a parent dropping their child
off with a list of dietary requirements,
a shoebox full of medication and half
a dozen emergency phone numbers

Following a sleepover at yours, your
child will be invited to one in return
and you will get a night off – hooray!

After an action-packed DVD
and a load of junk food, they
will be up half the night

SIGNS THAT YOUR CHILD IS WIELDING TOO MUCH POWER

You have to check with *them* what
time they want to go to bed

They've banned you from
parents' evening at school

They check your texts

They have a lock on the inside
of their bedroom door

HOW TO SPOT A SPOILT CHILD AT SCHOOL

For 'show and tell' they
bring in their Rolex

They're excused from games
due to a skiing injury

At lunchtime they send out for something
from their favourite restaurant

The chauffeur has his own parking
space in the playground

DOS AND DON'TS FOR THE SCHOOL LUNCHBOX

DO	DON'T
Give them something healthy	List the sugar, salt and fat content on the box
Make the food attractive	Crimp their sandwiches into animal shapes when they're 14
Try to follow any school guidelines	Go round the playground pointing out how fat and unhealthy some of the teachers look
Allow them one treat, such as a small chocolate bar	Imagine that chocolate oranges, sherbet lemons and strawberry shoelaces are part of their five a day

MOMENTS WHEN YOU SHOULD BE CONCERNED ABOUT YOUR KIDS

You realise the only book
they've read is Facebook

Their idea of a balanced diet is
a quarter-pounder burger and
a quarter pound o' sweets

Their texting thumb is the only part
of their body that gets any exercise

They're on alcopops when all their
friends are still on Coco Pops

WHAT WILL HAPPEN TO YOU WHEN YOUR CHILDREN BECOME TEENAGERS

Overnight you will become officially the stupidest person on Earth

You will suddenly lose any ability to dress fashionably

You will develop previously unrealised skills of being able to cause acute embarrassment

You will bear a striking
resemblance to a cashpoint

If you're interested in finding out more about our books, find us on Facebook at **Summersdale Publishers** and follow us on Twitter at @Summersdale.

www.summersdale.com